STIMULATING YOUR LITTLE ONE'S MIND

Everything you need to help your newborn discover the world

Written by Dominique van der Kaa

Translated by Rebecca Neal

Health and Wellbeing | 50MINUTES.com

50MINUTES.com

HEALTH AND WELLBEING
WITHOUT THE HEADACHE

STOP PROCRASTINATING - RIGHT NOW!
Beat your procrastination habit once and for all
NOW
Health and Wellbeing
50MINUTES.com

Make learning fun!

Learn to love yourself

Dealing with bullying at school

Your guide to making friends

www.50minutes.com

STIMULATING YOUR LITTLE ONE'S MIND

- **Problem:** as all parents know, the first few months in a newborn's life play a decisive role in their development and future. This means that it is vital to help your baby acquire the motor, intellectual and social skills they will need later on.
- **Aims:** to understand your newborn's psychomotor development and help them to discover the world.
- **FAQs:**
  - What should I do if my baby refuses to eat?
  - What toy should I choose for my child?
  - Are dummies useful?
  - How can I tell if I am overstimulating my baby?
  - My one-year-old is not speaking. Is this normal?
  - How can I know if my child's development is delayed?

While it is always good for parents to see their child develop and get excited about their environment, it is still important to make sure that they acquire their motor skills gradually, at their own pace. Rushing through the learning process could have serious consequences.

EMOTIONAL DEVELOPMENT

When babies are born, they already have emotional communication abilities. Initially, attachment to their mother develops through innate behaviours. Crying, sucking or grasping allow an infant to maintain physical contact with their mother and feel safe. At the start of a newborn's life, they are completely dependent on adults to satisfy their primary needs. Their sensory capacities are illustrated in their interactions with adults: they seek physical contact and caresses, and are calmed by their parents' voices. From the third week of life, the mother and her baby tend to look at one another. From a very early age, the infant's smile indicates their pleasure at being in contact with other people. Social smiling becomes selective at the age of three months.

If the people around the newborn respond appropriately to their demands, they will develop a feeling of security and a positive self-image, which will enable them to acquire new skills. However, if their needs are not satisfied, they will experience anxious attachment, lack self-confidence and mistrust others.

As infants grow up, they gradually become more independent and less attached to their mother. For this process of separation and physical distancing to go well, the child and their parents need to be emotionally in tune. In other words, successful detachment requires healthy attachment.

At the age of between two and three months, the first signs of dialogue emerge, with alternating roles. At the age of around six months, the baby's ability to imitate sounds allows this dialogue to develop further. At this age, newborns still look for contact with their mother and begins to do so more insistently. They also take a greater interest in their body and the objects around them. Finally, they look more closely at adults' faces and use cries to express unhappiness and anxiety.

As children can distinguish between familiar and unfamiliar faces between the age of eight and nine months, at this stage they will express their worries around strangers.

By the time a baby is about a year old, they will have acquired many new skills and will get a lot of enjoyment from moving around, mastering particular gestures and manipulating toys and objects. They still like being with their mother and experience a strong desire for her presence. When she does not respond, they feel sad and gradually come to realise that they cannot always make her come to them. They feel both powerful, when they experience pleasure, and powerless, when what they want differs from what the adult wants. At this age, they are also capable of giving objects to adults, so a new form of exchange is established. This results in the appearance of a series of new notions: frustration and permission, autonomy and dependence, give and take, and exchange and taking back.

Another thing that happens in this period is that infants derive pleasure from acquiring new skills by themselves and express their need for independence. They start saying "no" and imitating adult behaviour. The baby's personality starts to take shape, but they are still anxious at the idea of losing their parents' love. This fear can manifest itself as distress when the infant is told that they cannot do something or has trouble sleeping. They then want reassuring rituals to help them sleep (bedtime stories, nursery rhymes, lullabies) which require the presence of a parent. They mainly remain attached to their mother to deal with bodily needs or things that make them unhappy, but they can form bonds with other people.

HOW CAN YOU HELP YOUR BABY TO DEVELOP?

STIMULATING THEIR SENSES

Meals

An infant's food is a good way of developing their five senses. While newborns only consume milk (via breastfeeding or formula feeding) for the first four months of their life, a world of discovery opens up to them once solid or semi-solid foods are introduced.

Between the ages of four and six months, you can think about introducing a little variety into their diet, as long as their foods are all mixed into smooth purées. If your baby has allergies, or if you have a family history of allergies and intolerances, do not rush and wait until they have reached the age of six months. Feel free to ask your paediatrician for advice. Take it slowly and only introduce one new food at a time. Start with fruits and vegetables that you eat regularly: your child will already be familiar with them because they tasted them during your pregnancy.

However, taste is not the only sense that can be developed through meals. In fact, this is an ideal opportunity to appeal to all the senses. Give them food with a range of different colours and textures, encourage them to smell the things they are eating, and so on. Vary their diet as much as possible, because always giving them the same meals can lead not only to boredom, but also to a fear of new things.

If they refuse to eat certain foods, do not force them. Reintroduce the food they are afraid of in good conditions (in a relaxed atmosphere, through play, and so on), without hiding it and presenting it in a visually attractive way so that your baby will want to taste it. Never use a system of rewards and punishments, because this will condition your child to take advantage of the situation. Similarly, never praise your child for eating well, as this may lead them to overeat to try and please you.

It may be helpful to establish little rituals leading up to the meal: explain to your child what is happening, put a bib on them, show them the foods you are cooking, and so on. Mealtimes should be quality time for the child and their parents and should take place in a calm atmosphere.

Massage

Massaging your baby is a way of showing your affection through touch. However, you should not begin this practice before your newborn has reached the age of one month, because their belly button will not have healed until this point.

A new form of massage known as Shantala emerged in the 2000s. This is a traditional technique which aids the child's development through gentle support and a strong parent-child relationship. The technique was developed following an encounter between a Western obstetrician, Frédérick Leboyer (1918-2017), and a young Indian woman from Calcutta named Shantala, and involves massaging the different parts of your child's body, starting from the top and working down with small, gentle back and forth movements.

The many benefits of massage for your child's emotional, motor and sensory development are already well established:

- It stimulates the circulatory, lymphatic, digestive, respiratory and nervous systems, and can therefore be used to soothe colic and constipation, unblock the sinuses, clear the respiratory tract, and so on.
- It helps the baby to become more aware of their body and facilitates their psychomotor development by making them more agile, improving their muscle tone and allowing them to discover the world around them.
- It strengthens the emotional bond between the newborn and the person massaging them.
- It is a very effective relaxation method if it is carried out in a calm atmosphere.
- It results in an atmosphere which encourages communication. Furthermore, it involves exchanging words and smiles, making it a playful activity and facilitating the

acquisition of intellectual abilities.

- It involves direct contact between the baby and the person massaging them, which requires a degree of trust.

Other activities

Many everyday activities provide an opportunity to awaken your child's senses. The important thing is to make sure that you always respect their development and allow them to go at their own pace. For example, going for a walk is an excellent way of introducing them to the outside world and is recommended from a very early age. Bathtime is also an ideal time to share with your child and strengthen their sensory capacities.

DEVELOPING THEIR INTELLECTUAL CAPACITY

Language

It is very important to speak to your baby even if they cannot give you an intelligible response, because this will help them to develop their linguistic and mental capacities.

When parents talk to their children, they tend to speak in a higher voice than usual. Specialists call the register used to talk to babies motherese. This childlike language, which is characterised by slower delivery, marked intonation and childish vocabulary, in fact very closely resembles the language of the infant. This means that it captures their attention by appealing to their emotions. As the child's language skills develop and they gradually try to imitate the adult, this "baby talk" is gradually replaced by ordinary language, which allows the child to acquire vocabulary and syntax.

Below is some advice to stimulate your infant's language skills:

- respond to all their attempts at communication by smiling;
- talk to them whenever you are together (when you are changing them, bathing them or feeding them, for example);
- later on, avoid baby talk and use real words, enunciated clearly;
- emphasise your intonation;
- incorporate facial expressions and gestures into your communication;
- name everything that attracts their attention and that they touch;
- describe their surroundings, their actions and your actions;
- use simple instructions and short sentences;
- encourage interaction, which is the best time for developing language, by playing with them and giving them time to speak;
- repeat the words they try to pronounce back to them correctly.

QUICK TIP

Remember that nonverbal communication is also an effective way of helping your baby to develop their speech. When you talk to them, make sure that you are in a place where they can see you easily.

USING GAMES TO DEVELOP THEIR MOTOR AND EMOTIONAL SKILLS

Games can be used to stimulate all of the newborn's senses. Through these interactive activities, they find out about the world around them, learn to distinguish between different colours and shapes, are introduced to sounds and noises, and use their sense of touch to discover new textures.

As well as helping babies to understand their environment, games also play a role in their motor development. As an infant manipulates rattles, building blocks and mobiles, their movements and gestures become sharper and they learn to focus their attention.

Playing together

Newborns are capable of acquiring many skills for themselves under the right emotional conditions. In this way, they can develop their gross and fine motor skills and learn more about the people and objects around them. By playing with them, you will establish a relationship based on exchange and affection. Babies are happy when one of their parents devotes some time to them.

- Before the age of three months, playing will not be an integral part of your newborn's daily life. You can still stimulate them by using some gestures regularly, such as encouraging them to make a pedalling movement with their legs so that they can feel their body better, or carrying them in a sling, taking care to respect their physiological position.

- From the ages of three to six months, your infant will develop some sensory and motor capacities. It is now time to help them learn and stimulate their sense of hearing, for example by getting them to listen to a range of sounds, such as animal noises.
- By the time your child has reached the age of six to twelve months, they will have grown a lot. Now is the perfect time to introduce some games that will help them to develop their intellectual, motor and social skills. These games include chasing them on all fours, hide and seek, reading stories, improvising concerts and singing to them.
- Between the ages of one and two, a child will want to imitate their parents in their daily tasks. Let them help you prepare meals, do the dishes, fold the laundry or wipe down the table. These tasks will allow them to hone their movements and coordination and increase their self-confidence. The aim is not for them to carry out the tasks perfectly, but for them to enjoy being with you and accomplishing little gestures by themselves.

Parents all have different amounts of time to spend with their children. The important thing is not the number of hours you spend with your baby, but the quality of your time together.

Playing alone

Think about giving your child some time alone to observe their surroundings. Newborns do not always need an adult around to play with them, because they are capable of entertaining themselves for a certain period of time. Letting them play independently gives them the opportunity to express their creativity and potential. You can help them by creating an attractive, safe environment and leaving toys within reach. This alone time is very important for your child's development, because it allows them to get used to being by themselves and amuse themselves without adults. This will make separation healthier and less stressful later on.

The choice of toy

It is important to choose toys that are suitable for your baby's age and stage of development. They should be attractive and good quality in order to attract and hold their attention. There is no point giving them too many toys at once: limit their choice to three or four and, above all, respect their favourite toy, even if it is old, ugly or damaged (provided it is still safe, of course), because it will reassure and calm them.

Between the age of one and three months, infants are not very active. The main aim of toys is therefore to attract their attention and gently stimulate their senses. You should consider:

- Opting for toys with a clear contrast between black and

white, rather than colourful objects.
- Choosing toys that produce sounds or music to develop their hearing.
- Hanging a mobile above their cot. By following its movement with their eyes, your baby will improve their capacity for visual exploration.

From the age of three to six months, toys can be more interactive. For example, you could:

- put a mirror in front of your child so that they can look at themselves and get an overall view of the room they are in;
- lay them down on their stomach and put a toy by their side to encourage them to turn over onto their back;
- let them explore by giving them cubes made of different materials, rattles, toys that make sounds, little figurines or stuffed animals that are easy to grab hold of, and so on.

it will help them to concentrate and organise their activity.

By the age of six to twelve months, your child will have acquired a range of psychomotor skills and will need toys that are adapted to these new skills. You could give them:

- Toys that make sounds and emit light. They will soon learn that they can manipulate the toys to make them give off sound or light.
- Picture books, which have the advantage of being very interactive. Your child will be drawn to the different textures, colours, mirrors, and so on. These books will also help them to associate sounds and images with words.
- Stackable toys, which will develop their concentration and sense of observation and precision.

Between the age of twelve and eighteen months, the infant's motor skills will continue to develop and their intellectual capacities will become stronger. Toys which provide cultural enrichment and help them to develop their motor skills and intellectual abilities then become essential. Do not hesitate to:

- select toys that they can pull, push or roll (in other words, anything that encourages the child to move);
- opt for games which will develop their dexterity (sorting shapes or fitting them together, and so on);
- give them a ball to help them work on their balance and improve their coordination.

From the age of eighteen months to two years, children begin to reflect more. From this point, you should opt for educational games and games that let them play pretend, such as:

- games of skill,
- construction games,
- dolls, prams and lorries,
- miniature kitchens, supermarkets or garages.

SUPPORTING YOUR CHILD'S DEVELOPMENT AND PREPARING THEM FOR THE FUTURE

EARLY EDUCATION

Early education is vital for your child, because it allows them to come out of their shell, discover new things and prepare to socialise, while respecting their pace of development.

Children need limits. This rule also applies to infants, who are at an age when they want everything right now. Your baby is curious and has not yet learned patience, so your role as parents is to get them used to the word "no" and to put in place a system of rules which will help them to develop at their own pace and remain considerate of others.

How can I go about this?

If you want to give your child a healthy and effective early education, it is important to remain firm and calm. You need to demonstrate positive authority by gently explaining to your child that there are rules to follow, and that there will be consequences if they break them. Reprimanding your child should never mean just shouting at them or sending them to their room or the naughty step. Instead, talk to them and make sure they understand that what they did was wrong and that they need to apologise and think about their actions. It is important to make sure that punishment does not go on for too long. This will make it easier for them to learn what they can and cannot do at home and elsewhere.

Below are some tips to help you set limits and supervise your child's early education:

- Respect their pace and structure their day with little rituals to reassure them.
- Do not rush to their room at the first sign of tears if all their needs have been satisfied. Instead, wait a while to see if they calm down by themselves.
- Make them wait a bit before giving them the item they want and refuse if it could be dangerous for them, making sure to explain why.
- Put a rewards system in place – except for meals. This is an integral part of early education, but it must be spontaneous and justified. Avoid conditional rewards like "you could have… if…".
- Teach them manners by encouraging them to say "hello", "goodbye", "please", "thank you", "excuse me", and so on.
- Get them used to waiting their turn and do not give in to their tantrums.
- Avoid negative phases, because before the age of two children do not understand negation. If you say "Don't climb on the sofa!", they will hear "climb" and "sofa" and do it even if you tell them not to again. Instead, word the instruction as "Get down from the sofa!"
- Only ask them to do one thing at a time. Children can only retain one action, so there is no point giving them several instructions at once.
- Make things easier for them by speaking clearly and simply and using gestures. Until the age of two, children

have sensory-motor perception and are therefore more sensitive to gestures than words.

Do not forget that, if you have a partner, you should educate your child as a couple. Parents should maintain a united front and not contradict one another on their educational principles.

HOW SHOULD I DEAL WITH A PSYCHOMOTOR DELAY OR A DISABILITY?

Problems with psychomotor development can often be painful and worrying, both for the child and for their parents. Adapting the infant's education to their needs and helping them to deal with this learning difficulty on a daily basis therefore becomes a priority.

It is even more important to offer the child reassuring reference points and different spaces for each activity: a place to sleep, to wash, to eat and to play. This will make it easier for them to understand what is expected of them based on where they are.

It also helpful to know that the brain is very sensitive to external influences during the first three years of a child's life. This is known as neuroplasticity. It allows brain structures that are not yet determined to develop a specific function when they come into contact with their environment. Early and regular treatment can therefore influence and develop the child's capacities. There are support services with specialists who can help the parents and their child to manage this disability through adapted structures and methods.

Some therapeutic approaches

- **Neuropediatric physiotherapy** aims to develop the functional movement of children with motor disabilities. Two methods are frequently used as part of this approach: the Bobath concept and the Le Metayer method. The Bobath concept aims to assist with the child's sensory and motor development. It helps them to adapt their postures and movements in order to carry out functional activities and play as normally as possible. The Le Metayer method opts to re-educate the child through all their activities, while taking their difficulties into account.
- **Snoezelen**, also known as **controlled multisensory environment**, is a concept which originated in the Netherlands and offers sensory stimulation. Snoezelen rooms are designed to engage all the senses. The therapist only intervenes to help the child discover the activity, for example by placing an object within their reach or guiding them towards another activity if they show an interest in it. This nonverbal communication forges a relationship with the adult, and the infant emerges from their solitude to find a sense of wellbeing.
- **Speech-language pathology** helps the child to develop their oral language and suggests nonverbal forms of communication depending on their abilities. This therapeutic approach is also very effective in treating problems with eating and swallowing, in particular thanks to exercises which strengthen the muscles of the upper digestive organs such as the tongue and the pharynx.
- **Relational and global psychomotricity** helps the child to communicate with their body. It uses play in an envi-

ronment that makes the child feel safe.

As part of their development, your baby will discover more about other people and their environment, and will also gradually learn about themselves. Every new experience will help them to come out of their shell and broaden their horizons. To ensure your child's healthy development, you must let them go at their own pace and avoid pushing them too hard. When you are helping your child to discover new things, think about the limits to their skills and bear in mind the time when they developed their new abilities.

FAQS

WHAT SHOULD I DO IF MY BABY REFUSES TO EAT?

First of all, check that they are not sick. If they are otherwise well, do not force them to eat: a healthy child will never let themselves starve. Meals should be an opportunity to spend quality time with your baby. By forcing them to eat, you will turn this time into a source of conflict. Respecting your child means respecting their tastes too, so give them time to adapt. Just because they are refusing to eat something now does not mean they will keep on refusing. Offer them something else, taking care to present it attractively and telling them what it is. Finally, give your child fruit and vegetables to play with so that they get used to them and want to taste them.

WHAT TOY SHOULD I CHOOSE FOR MY CHILD?

It is vital that you choose toys that are suitable for your child's age and level of development and that catch their attention. During their first months, the games should be sensory, then movement-based, and finally educational. You should also like the toy, and it should be easy to use and safe. Look for CE marking, which shows that the toy conforms to European regulations, and the Lion Mark, a symbol used in Britain to show that toys are safe and high quality. Finally, never take their favourite toy away from them, because it reassures them and calms them down.

ARE DUMMIES USEFUL?

Dummies should only be used as a last resort. While children can find them comforting and calming as long as they have a sucking reflex, they can also do more harm than good.

If you give them their dummy at the first sign of a problem, not only will they get into the habit of always looking for comfort from someone or something else, but you will not necessarily solve the issue. If you give them a bit of time, they will find a way to calm themselves down.

The other danger of dummies is that they maintain the sucking reflex, which can delay the passage to adult chewing and swallowing, as well as the appearance of speech, because this follows on from the ability to swallow. Over the longer term, using dummies can lead to occlusion problems and problems with the positioning of the teeth.

HOW CAN I TELL IF I AM OVERSTIMULATING MY BABY?

Newborns pay attention and take part in games as long as they are enjoying them. Their joy is spontaneous and clearly visible. Your child's behaviour will let you know if you are overstimulating them: they will be tired or sleepy, stop paying attention, cry, and so on. All these little signs will tell you it is time to stop.

MY ONE-YEAR-OLD IS NOT SPEAKING. IS THIS NORMAL?

Do not worry: all children develop at their own pace, and in many cases this delay is not a sign of anything serious. Most children say their first words between the ages of ten and fifteen months, string two words together at around eighteen months and form short sentences by the age of around two. However, this is not always the case: if your child is not speaking yet, they may be focusing on other skills, such as learning to walk.

However, there are some signs which should give you pause and make you think about consulting a paediatrician: your child does not react to noise; they get regular ear, nose and throat infections; they struggle to understand; they do not use their finger to point at the objects they want; they do not try to communicate; and so on.

HOW CAN I KNOW IF MY CHILD'S DEVELOPMENT IS DELAYED?

You need to look at a premature baby's development based on their corrected age for the first two years of their life. This is the age your baby would be if they had been born at full term. It is calculated as follows: corrected age = chronological age − number of weeks early. For example, a 6-month-old premature baby born after 28 weeks of pregnancy will have a corrected age of 3 months (6 months − 12 weeks). Their developmental age should therefore correspond to their corrected age rather than their chronological age.

If they are lagging behind in terms of skills, do not hesitate to consult your paediatrician: they will be able to find the cause of this delay and suggest suitable treatments and follow-up care.

We want to hear from you!
Leave a comment on your online library
and share your favourite books on social media!

FURTHER READING

BIBLIOGRAPHY

- D'Audiffret, C. and D'Audiffret, A. (2011) *L'art de vivre en famille(s)*. Paris: Éditions de l'Atelier.
- Bourrillon, A. and Benoist, G. (2013) *Pédiatrie. Réussir les épreuves classantes nationales*. Paris: Elsevier Masson.
- De Broca, A. (2006) *Le développement de l'enfant : aspects neuro-psycho-sensoriels*. Paris: Elsevier Masson.
- Browne, J. V. (2008) Chemosensory Development in the Fetus and Newborn. *Newborn and Infant Nursing Reviews*, volume 8, pp. 180-186.
- Ferland, F. (No date) Jouer avec bébé. *Naître et grandir*. [Online]. [Accessed 7 July 2017]. Available from: <http://naitreetgrandir.com/fr/etape/0_12_mois/fiches-activites/fiche.aspx?doc=bg-naitre-grandir-jouer-bebe>
- Landrieu, P. and Tardieu, M. (2001) *Neurologie pédiatrique*. Paris: Elsevier Masson.
- Le Métayer, M. (1999) *Rééducation cérébro-motrice du jeune enfant. Éducation thérapeutique*. Paris: Elsevier Masson.
- Maury, M. (No date) Développement affectif du nourrisson. L'installation précoce de la relation mère-enfant et son importance. *Faculté de médecine de Toulouse*. [Online]. [Accessed 7 July 2017]. Available from: <http://www.medecine.ups-tlse.fr/dcem3/module03/08.DEVELOPPEMENTAFFECTIF(3-3.pdf>
- Place, M-H. (2012) *60 activités Montessori pour mon bébé*. Paris: Nathan.
- De Truchis, C. (2009) *L'éveil de votre enfant : le tout-petit*

au quotidien. Paris: Éditions Albin Michel.

• Valleteau de Moulliac, J., Gallet, J-P. and Chevalier, B. (2005) *Guide pratique de la consultation en pédiatrie*. Paris: Elsevier Masson.

ADDITIONAL SOURCES

• Atkins, L. (2009) *First-Time Parent: The honest guide to coping brilliantly and staying sane in your baby's first year*. London: HarperCollins.
• Kavanagh, W. (2005) *Baby Touch: Massage and Reflexology for Babies and Children*. London: Hamlyn.
• Kramer Arsenault, C. (2017) *Newborn 101*. New York: The Experiment.
• Leboyer, F. (1997) *Loving Hands: The Traditional Art of Baby Massage*. New York: Newmarket Press.

IMPROVE YOUR GENERAL KNOWLEDGE

IN A BLINK OF AN EYE !

www.50minutes.com